THE
SALAMANDER
MIGRATION

THE SALAMANDER

University of Pittsburgh Press

MIGRATION

AND OTHER POEMS

Cary Waterman

Published by the University of Pittsburgh Press, Pittsburgh, Pa., 15260
Copyright © 1980, Cary Waterman
All rights reserved
Feffer and Simons, Inc., London
Manufactured in the United States of America

Library of Congress Cataloging in Publication Data

Waterman, Cary, 1942–
    The salamander migration.

    (Pitt poetry series)
    I. Title.
PS3573.A814S2   811'.5'4   79-24291
ISBN 0-8229-3415-9
ISBN 0-8229-5315-3 pbk.

Acknowledgment is made to the following publications, which first published some of the poems in this book: *Dacotah Territory; First Thaw; Moons and Lion Tailes; Northeast; Poets On: Loving; Sing, Heavenly Muse; Tendril;* and *Westend.*

"Homecoming" originally appeared in *Bloodroot,* no. 6 (Spring 1979).

"Jumping with My Daughter" appeared first in *25 Minnesota Poets #2* and again in *Connections Magazine.*

I would like to thank the Bush Foundation of Minneapolis for a grant which made possible the writing of this book.

*The publication of this book is supported by grants
from the National Endowment for the Arts
in Washington, D.C., a Federal agency,
and the Pennsylvania Council on the Arts.*

At seventy-three I began to understand the true construction of animals, plants, trees, birds, fishes and insects. At ninety I will enter into the secrets of things. At one hundred and ten everything —every dot, every dash—will live.

—Hokusai

For My Mother
Emily Siebert Brown

CONTENTS

CONTENTS

Homing

ME, LEARNING TO DANCE

I don't know how.
And so you pose before me,
a right angle,
a cock-eyed telephone pole
ready to begin.

Mother watches, approving.
She is tiny.
I am tiny.
And you are so much bigger,
weaving like Goliath
in the space before me.

And then we start this strangeness,
bobbing and heaving like heavy ducks.
Right, left,
right, right, left.
You going one way,
me following like an afterthought.
Steam swirls from our heads
as we circle the small room
ten minutes before my date arrives.

But it is too late.
Here he is with a corsage box,
two tiny pink tea roses squeezed
by the gregarious carnations.
And I go off with him into the night,
into his car.

And I do not love him.
It is you I love.
But I will never tell you,
never tell you,
never.

3

AFTER A DEATH

You have planted Irish heather,
purple by the rocks.
And funkia, the green and white plant
of poverty in the soil,
and wetness and sunlessness.
And you have cultivated also
the sexual holly,
such stiff leaves glossy
with love.

You tell me how my father
would count the trees
as he walked the lot in evening.
Counting maple, pine,
and sassafras, the mitten-leaved tree.
How he would stop before the huge elm
rotting at the boundary line
and dominating everything,
its roots reaching toward
the house foundation.

You will have it cut down,
the massive trunk,
the branches filled with words of disease,
hanging over the porch, garage,
the new flower bed.
You will drive out the black ants
who have gathered there in families,
and who are now making
longer and longer explorations,
leaving odor trails all the way
to the back door of this house.

SKIING WITH MY DAUGHTERS

They are up the hill
ahead of me,
straight up into the white ice
of a young girl's mind.
I scramble after them,
bigger, browner,
heavier in the snow.
I pull all the things
I think they will need.

They are at the top
before me
and leave immediately,
twisting down the narrow trail,
bouncing like rabbits
through the ruts.
I am amazed.
They are still on their feet.
I lean forward,
yell forward,
take the bitter wind into
my mouth.

Then they're gone.
They have left me alone
above timberline.
I am standing at the top
without any impulse
to descend.

THE LESSON

The young rabbits stumble
from their gray fur
yellow grass nest
woven into this pocket
of earth.

Then they fall before
our dogs
who are only killing time
this long summer evening.

You run and take them
although they are hanging limp
and broken,
the blood running loose inside.
And together
we put them in a shoe box,
make it soft,
make it quiet.

And then we sit
on the porch swing,
the box between us
watching how long it takes
for something to die,
seeing how hard it is,
the mouth flown open
always for more.

And now it is your turn
to cry,
to be angered.
The dogs at our feet.
The long summer light.

HOMECOMING

Up talking until three.
It is owl time.
It is the same every visit,
and the forgotten seeds rain down,
every time the same ones
shaped like pine needles and filling
up the furrows of our backs.

This is the company we keep.
Face to face we will not see
love darkening on the forest floor.
Will not see the old words
like the woodcutter's hands
splitting us further and further
into separate nights.

In the morning blooms the light
from some place we do not visit yet,
making less heavy on our faces
the lines of wilderness
we carry into day.

Making less heavy
the things we do not say.

VISITING THE CEMETERY
IN BRIDGEPORT, CONNECTICUT

The bodies of immigrants
settle for the last time
in official rows.
It is as crowded here
as it was in steerage,
the Irish and the Germans
untranslatable
in the single language
of death.

There are few visitors,
few who come to see
this ocean of tombstones,
the stone trees,
and the stone colored pigeons
picking through the summer grass.

My family lies in
narrow beds.
I wander among them
discovering like driftwood
the names I remember,
the ones I forgot.

Lizzie, Rose,
Annie, Bridgit, all
the beautiful sisters,
their long red hair once braided,
their light dresses folded with promises.
And the husbands beside them.

Peter, John,
and Charles, my grandfather
who would not talk when he got old,
who traded a German village
for washing floors in the Bridgeport hospital,
for the dull slosh of the mop,
never saying how much it cost him.

JUMPING WITH MY DAUGHTER

after reading of a woman who was killed by jumping from a burning
tenement while holding her eleven-year-old daughter

Hugging,
we fly down the air,
our breath dragging
one step behind us.
I push you above me like a lover.
My body is the last rung of the ladder,
the bottom step before the light.

If only we were
lighter than fire.
If only we could circle the gutter,
two nighthawks cackling before dark.

But you are heavier than blood.
You are the living room rug
that smothers and buries me.

And I am your plate of bones,
a pillow of skin.
Where we land I slip away from you finally,
my lap spreading out between your fingers
and into the street.

GETTING OLD

You take pills
and have coughing fits at dark.
I have two ocean currents
deepening their routes around my mouth.
Our children look at us secretly.
They know we cannot tell anymore
what they are thinking.

We grow old together,
two butternut husks collected
at the roots of the same tree.
In the marriage blender
we have been set on chip.
Pieces fell away
and dried like the snipped ends of beans.

Things continue to fall from us now—
skin,
children,
ambitions.
They transform themselves
to a life on their own,
forgetful,
and mute.

FOR BRIDGIT GROWING UP

This hard life
of yours
makes a hardness also
in my breasts
as if the milk
still came
warm and blue for sucking,
as if it had not curdled
long ago
into an absence.

You have learned the dreams
by heart—
freedom and
equality.
They are like a pair of shoes
you tie on before going to meet
the others.

Then how suddenly
it happens
that the real life
slams against you
insisting it will
be let in,
insisting it will have
its hard way with
all of us.

Now there is so much
you do not like,
so many you rage against
like a stubbed cedar
in the wind.
And we do not help much,
fingering the beads
of discipline,
doling it out
like small change
from our pockets.

And oh
how your skin begins
to rust with adolescence
preparing in the night
for the stiff morning
that will assail you
and do its damndest
to bow you down.

DEATH ON THE FARM

Halfway between the house and the barn
there is a dead Holstein dairy cow,
black and white like a map of the world.
She is big eared and square toothed
and frozen solid.

Who ever said death was fluid
and wore long garments like a wind?
Death is a pile.
The truck from the rendering kitchen
should have been here days ago.
Now it is too late.
The cow is beginning to come back to life.
I can see her breathing from the window.

She looks comfortable there
even though the dogs have begun chewing a dark hole
that will end at the heart.
After they come to take her,
after her fingered milk bag,
her white braced hips are gone,
her breathing will go on in that place.
Up and down against the soft weeds,
in and out,
filling with water the dark space
that goes between us
when we are not even looking.

Domestications

MORNING

In the morning
a yellow slap of light
reaches around the clouds.

I am awake.
I want something good
to hold me in
like the silken strings
on the sky diver's
parachute.

But instead I continue
to fall down into the day,
away from the intelligence
of dreams,
the faithfulness to dark.
The day reaches through me
for voices and food.

Wait.
I hear its mouth
slip over the doorknob,
its fist begin to knock.

HOW WE LIVE

I push myself up and go to work on the flower beds, digging, feeling my back in it, pulling stubble, the dead winter away for burning. I dig and dig, thinking of the rough night of dreams. One in which a child died and I slammed myself shut, refusing to admit pain. And then the second dream of a child, who puts a small animal, a chipmunk maybe, on my shoulder. The chipmunk rests there and then suddenly flies out to hide in the tall grass. Then he returns, slowly, to lie down by me, to be petted, rolling over beside me, turning his soft, protected belly up toward the light.

I have worked my way toward where the tiger lilies are waking from their shallow beds. And still digging, digging, I raise suddenly one large clump of earth, and turn up to the sun dozens of small white bulbs, like eggs, their first shoots hidden under the dirt.

And we are stopped there. I hold them to the air and they startle back at the light and the release. Then I rush to push them back, back down, pressing them into their bed, trying to return them untouched, underground, safe. Since this is not the time to separate for growing, to cut away the corded roots, destroy what is diseased. And neither one of us is ready for this rupture, this birth into sight, this sudden clashing of air, and earth, and light.

TRIPTYCH

for Karen

I

We loosen conversation
          down around our shoulders.
Our children have been nightgowned
          and caressed.
They slip through to sleep easily,
          thread stitching them into velvet.

Cast in this maternity we are
          the image and the weaver
spinning words into night fabric.
          This panel of the tapestry
begins the tentative song that has been
          sighing through all ages.

II

These are the bone-clean hours
          when friendship bares itself
like an orbiting moon
          unmolested by the daylight.
We talk to each other all night,
          threading jasmine and bloodroot
in the fields between our words.

We are stitching the story together again,
          making a poultice of language
to soothe the sores of our isolation.
          Outside, the circle of the night
lays out flat around us like thread
          knotted from the piecework of centuries,
each section a finger's length of women's labor.

III

Convalescence brings us to dawn.
        The light is changed here and
our words slide by sparkling like sea swells.
        A hunger that was thinness in our ribs
vanishes out of the morning.

From this night working of thread and fabric,
        women's words stitching a birth into each death,
you turn your head among the morning lilies.

The light moves in rivulets
        all around us.

ELDERBERRY JAM

You have been gone hours
foraging in the woods
behind our house.
In your absence
the night came and stood
at the back door.

Now you come back,
stand in the doorway,
your hair wet with dew.
And in your hand
a brown bag in which
the elderberries are captive,
still rigid,
still resisting on
their hooks of stem.

After we clean them
I start the jam.
In an old pot
the berries burst into purple.
They are like little skulls of stain.
I add sugar,
that white iceberg,
and a scant touch of water
to start the boil.
Now the fruit is becoming tender,
the juice begins to flow.

At the moment of mashing
they rise up
vengefully,
shaking fists,

boiling and turning
like hot rock
and pushing to the center,
to smother,
to go down
in the purple face of the pot.

And the night
how it comes into the kitchen,
surrounds us,
pouring down through
the rusty screens.

WANT

When I want
it's right now.
I want to perch on top of it,
dig my toenails in,
climb and pick the bananas.

We don't
always want the same thing.
Sometimes you want to go
underground
while I want to explode like dust
between particles of air.

If I say
want,
want,
want
I have three heads,
the three Gorgons.

But want wants to grow.
It wants to be a daisy with thorns.
It wants to be have and did.
It wants to swallow all the other words.

And I want to get fat and sassy
like a blues singer.
I want to be Billie Holiday
and Janis Joplin.
I want to be cut up
and bled with leeches.

Sometimes I want
to tear want apart
and see if there is nothing
in its heart.

Want can be so sad
I can twist it around a razor
and it wouldn't say anything but
hurt,
hurt,
hurt.

Hurt is not like want.
It lives forever
by itself
in a small tin box.

LAUNDROMAT

It would be better
to be at the river
where we could touch
the curling lips of sun.
Our babies wrapped snug
would melt their
strong small arms
across our backs.
And we would dance,
bending and rising from
the old stones,
those volcanic faces
that have become like sisters
from years of rubbing out
afterbirth
and death.

In the laundromat
everything breaks.
Glass and lights
and machines with springs
and screws
and the fierce red faces
of motors
that twist and whine
into this box
of fluorescent light.
The only dance is hurry
to load,
unload and fold,
the cheap seams unravelling
in their quick dark furrows.

The new mothers come here,
poorness dripping from their hair.
And their babies cry
or stare
or lay propped with bottles,
with plastic nipples
to muffle them against
their loneliness.
And there is no pleasure
except for the frayed clothes
dancing together like dolphins
in the huge dryers.
And the money man
who empties our quarters from
each machine
and starts them touching one another
in the bottom of his dark bag.

MONDAY, MONDAY

The impatiens grows
spindly
and almost leafless
to the top of the window.

Living inside
on diffused light
it suffers from dry rot
and selflessness.

Monday washes by.
Unnoticed.

It is wearying,
the same two eyes,
a pair of speechless plants,
the predictable window light.

I thirst
to say something
of myself
that will include everything,
taproots
and pollen dances.

I want to be
a hammered wedge
splitting
the dry fingers of wood.

An iron tongue
rushing
into someone else's life.

THE FARMER'S WIFE

The land is taut
and presses on me this summer,
stretched like dry skin across
the forehead.

I watch my husband from
the kitchen window
make row after practiced row,
finger straight,
as straight as his love
and leading always in the same
direction,
all toward the same boundary line.
The day unfolds like a bolt of gauze.

But beside him at night
I dream only of ships
and learn the escape route of water,
searching through the endless canals
for the inland sea,
the whitecapped wave that will open
the door to weightlessness.

Then every morning it is there again,
the sun stroked fields asking for my hand
as if another marriage should take place.
As if I were a drowning woman,
one hand surrounding the rootless clam,
the other scratching for a shore
where men stand poised to cultivate
with rakes and hoes.

DRIVING TO TOWN
AT NIGHT WITH THE DOG

Cloudy dark.
A skunk pushing into the tall grass.
Your nose goes on alert.
Ah, if we had rolled over him.

And now something else,
very small with eyes as bright as lockets
crouched by the side of the road.

A car comes up on us fast,
swerves out to pass
and shoots on down the highway.

You flex your hairy paws.
Your ears lift and settle with sounds
I do not hear.
Then the store and lights
and you wait outside for me like a moon.

Now our skin is shadowing
against the windshield again.
Our eyes are spread to black holes
in the dark light.

All the way there
and all the way back
and you do not say a word.

WORK POEM

She slides from the pitcher of night,
dreams lost in the sun rush of morning,
and in the quiet fury of the breakfast table.
There is no love between the eggs
frying in the fat of a pan,
in the juice squeezed by hand
from every orange.

The work of the spider.
She comes and goes all day
colliding only with herself,
her two brains, two hands
conducting the dishwater in
its greasy song.

Uncounted words of light
spread across the ground like semen,
spilled, not to be.
But tonight she will go with food
to the dog who is healing himself,
licking his scabs in the star darkened barn.

She will look into the trees on the way.
The trees and their voices.
Each one filling completely
its own well of darkness.

AFTER THE PIG BUTCHERING

What does the pig think of the dawn?
They do not sing but they hold it up.
—Pablo Neruda

I go back two days later
for the skin.
It is dismal weather.
The floor of the shed is wet
where blood mingles with the red paint
and the dark soft manure.
It is a watercolor of confusion and pain,
of the loss of a piece of thought.
The feeding pans are in chaos,
tipped like crazy men around the corners.

I have gone back to pick up the skin.
We left the entrails to droop in a compost heap.
I see them sinking like heat into the ground.
I know parts of them are ovaries.
And there are two blue-lipped stomachs
that seem to smile at me.
The skin is on the roof of the shed.

Carrying it I can tell that it weighs
about as much as my five-year-old son.
It is solid like a head against my breasts.
I begin to like carrying it and squeeze it closer,
rub my cheek into it,
and touch the taut nipples.
They are watchtowers
on both sides of the river we cut open.
I am bringing it home.

Now the smell is on me;
grease on my hands.
I bring it all into my house.
It slides around the doors,
under the beds.
It is pungent
and obsessive.

HARVESTING

This is the silence of full spaces.
Time and the fall conspire against us.
And there is sadness in the harvested fruit,
sadness in all the children sitting
at the silence of heavy desks.

Sometimes I do not know what we do.
Sometimes I do not know where
the sadness comes from
and for what purpose.

But tonight I will prepare a stew.
I will pick the longest carrots
drunk on their own fulfillment.
I will pick a finale of onions,
a wheelbarrow of potatoes.

We will sit down together.
We will begin again,
all of us,
all over again.

Breaking the Still Life

TEMPTATION

after a painting by Bouguereau

The constant presence of an enemy makes for the opposite of innocence.
—Anaïs Nin, *The Diary, IV*

The artist has trudged a long way
for this landscape into which
he will place his women.
He has puffed uphill carrying
that dented paint box
and a lightweight, brand-new easel,
a gift from his newest lover.

Or perhaps this scenery
is merely a backdrop
rolled down on oilcloth,
before which he poses his two models
so that he can then pose himself
before it all with beret and paintbrush
and yellow teeth.
Whichever is the reality, there is
the cleanness of summer,
a particular haze in the background
that lightly rubs itself over the hills.
And on the grass a naked girl-child.

Someone has tied a blood red ribbon
to hold back her curls.
She is caught for all time
parting the grass with her declarative fingers
which are only beginning to speak.
The woman beside her is clothed,
heavily, except for her sexual feet
which were the last part of her body to be born,
and which rub against each other
like bass swimming through the French grasses.
She is holding the ripe apple
like a globe of the world in her hands.

Water lilies suck mud
at the edge of the pond
as the child turns to the woman
who is perhaps an older sister
or a maid from the kitchen
who has been given the afternoon off.
They know that all our sins
are original and that
there is no temptation here
but to eat a late summer apple,
teeth thundering through
the red skin and white juice
to reach the seeds at the center
while a foolish man stands
with his back to all the light.

Now the artist has heard the dinner bell
ringing across the fields,
or perhaps only up the winding stairs
to his garret.
He descends toward evening
leaving them there,
descends toward a supper of boiled cabbage
and thin slices of tender lamb.

PERSPECTIVE

The black cat. Out prowling all night. At dawn he comes back, scratching, crying to be let in. You go to the door, wakened from a dream you cannot quite touch. You notice how much thinner he is. How, in these early hours, his face scars stand out in relief, like symbols cut into stone. Like petroglyphs you have to study. That you need to decipher.

They tell of the fire scratched nightly into the body. Of the passion for sleeplessness. You wonder at the half-chewed gopher under the tree. You know it is only a thin veneer of habit that brings the cat back every morning.

Inside the lighted kitchen he enters the family again and opens the black jaws of his brain for milk. Then turning, he hollowly rubs his side up against the Saint Bernard who has wakened also from a dream. Who has looked into the cold eyes of pilgrims circling higher and higher up into the light of mountain snow.

COMING BACK FROM THE FRONT LINES

I cross my arms,
let my cold hands swim up
like spawning salmon
inside the sleeves of this sweater.

The rest of my body
might suffer.
The head with its infinite
calculations.
And the thoughtless feet.
Even the belly although
it is the softest
and most hidden.
But the suffering of hands
would mean the end of love,
a shriveling of white light.

If I hold my hands to my face
certain empty afternoons
I can see the network again,
the lives like fossils in amber
pressed into my palms.
The crosshatch of the life line,
the tributaries of love.

Looking into my hands I see
that it is spring, raining.
The roads are rutted with mud.
Heavy guns and high wheeled carts
filled with wounded
go single file, creaking.
They all lead south,
all coming back from the front lines
of a war fought in winter
in which many others have died.

40

WAITING

for Phebe

I wait because it seems good to do,
to dismiss the notion of clouds
for the mysterious light inside them.

If what we know is any indication
the world must be falling in at the center
like a house bulldozed in the night.

You discover it while going to work the next morning,
the house with its face turned away from you now,
its body flat to the ground.
No one was a witness.

That happens to women I know.
A brace gives way
and the heart crumbles first.
Then veins and breasts.
And finally the hands, holding nothing,
laying flat at the sides like wet flags.

I am holding on to waiting for you today.
I am holding on to the clouds and the way they have of
burning themselves clear
from the inside out.

OCTOBER FOG

Looking out
late into morning
scarves of fog
wrap around the outbuildings.
It is impossible to see
the shivering cars on the highway.
Or the green cornpicker
in the next field.
After working all night
it sits humming the song of complacency.

Even the winter trees hide
their beginning
of stark needles and denial.

Then how it all changes!
In three breaths
a curve of road comes
and the farm trucks visibly fatten.

The trees clear shadows
from their brown throats.

And I hear the dog
barking across the brittle woodlot
at whatever private thing it is
that moves out of sight.

SUNDAY EVENING

It is a mistake to think that God is primarily concerned with religion.
—Archbishop of Canterbury

After supper the sun
still has hours left,
hours to bless whatever life
continues to turn sunward
on its stem.
You and I
bicycle up the road
through the absence of
our farmer neighbors
who have emptied Sunday
into the church of Martin Luther.

We ride past their livestock
whose ears are tipped with sun.
And past the heads of grain
designing a field that stretches
west to the horizon.

We bike for miles
with our dogs behind,
then in front,
then behind again.
The sun genuflects
over the rim.

And then you stop
to pick the sun's flowers
in the road ditch.
Jerusalem artichoke,
the flowers turning to the sun.
Your body bends
in an arch of light.

43

Out in the field
blackbirds lift up and fly west
like the Chinese word
for order.

SMALL COMFORTS

After relighting the fire
I come to sit on the cat's perch
that is on the third stair
by the east window
where there is sun
draining through the glass
this morning.

The cat sits looking out
the south window,
then back into the room
composing a thin idea
of comfort.
His tail is curled
across his forepaws
like a gate.

From my window there is snow
shadowed by ridges
and footprints.
And there are the winter trees
pulling themselves together
in shallow inhalings.

And there are
last summer's snapdragons
and marigolds
thrusting up their brittle
holographs
in snow
and 17 below.

FOR ALL THE DEAD DOGS

For all the dogs
with tires through their eyes,
with asphalt torn into
the blood lines
of their soft tipped ears.
For all the dogs
shoveled off the highway
and dumped in plastic bags,
in ditches.

These dead are folding into
themselves so that they grow
invisible like the trees concealed
in the pages of the Bible;
invisible like buffalo,
the ghost herds we only hear
behind our eyes.

*

Now this poem
is in your way.
If you are traveling
like mad
in the express lane—
run it down.
It will only be an accident.
Or if you want the skin
for a lap rug—
shoot it.
Between its eyes.

See the small breaths squeezed out,
leaving the mouth like fingertips,
touching you,
identifying everyone.

BREAKING THE STILL LIFE

This light comes in to circle the fall marigolds
drowsing on the varnished desk.
This morning light burns like sulphur
through the clouds
and through the children who also
waken cloudy from the frame of night.

The great light walks into morning
carrying dark asleep in its elbow.
It is a bursting of fruit.
It is the way the purple grapes dangle
from the white trellis.

The light raises us up from
the dream crib.
It says, go out,
become that which is not you,
what you have not touched,
never dreamed.

Inside the polished frame
our still life is broken.
Blue day-bowl and fruit and we
slip past the edges
toward the bright mouths of birds.

Migrations

THE SALAMANDER MIGRATION

for K.

Stopped by the emptiness I see approaching
in the bowl of the midwestern afternoon,
I wait, watch the day
polish itself down to a fine powder.
You are leaving tomorrow for Albuquerque,
following the husband you love
and do not love.
Bringing with you the girl-child
that has sprung up
like a prayer wheel,
a mushroom,
a stone.

Now you come to say good-bye,
to sit on my front porch surrounded
by fall burning itself up
in funeral pyres.
Together we snip the ends from
the last harvest of beans.
And together we watch the salamanders,
those black commas crawling
pregnant and slow
across the decaying road and
down into the creek bed.
They are solitary, like water,
not holding back,
and leaving nothing behind them.

In this season all life is fire
moving toward hibernation.
And soon you will drive the highway
between our houses one last time,

crying and veering to miss the salamanders,
their heavy rope bodies that carry
the next year inside them,
so that they might return
and return and return.

LOVE POEM

for M.

I. New Jersey, 1959

Morning settles in
through the windows.
We are so young,
two girls as graceful as
the leatherbound books
silently arranged in your father's study.

We read together
following Joyce through
the poorness of Dublin,
Thomas Mann into the family
of *Buddenbrooks.*
And finally Hesse
probing, dissecting
the heart of *Steppenwolf.*

And still we do not suspect a loss,
still we love each other,
growing up together
our vines braided on
the same trellis of light.

Beyond our windows
the seabirds seek from the shore
the long days of summer.
And we turn in this last peace,
sensing the slight blue wind
and our own faithfulness.

And we hear a few miles off
in the Atlantic
the shells turning also
over and over into memory.

II. Minnesota, 1978

Who betrayed us?
And when finally did we
betray each other,
sealing ourselves off
in the rain forest of domestication?

You have gone long ago
across one continent
and one ocean
to live in the shadow of Joyce's tower.
I have come here
where tonight mist rises from
the prairie of Minnesota
and rubs its thumbs against my window.

We have lost each other.
We do not speak of how we are
both encircled by children
as light as floating candles,
of the bondage of small loves growing,
of pain that is as plentiful as grass.

I only hear secondhand
you will have a new baby,
and that you keep honey bees
near your old stone house.
And that you are thin,
thin, and smoke too much,
striking match on match for fire.

DREAMING DROWNING

in a landlocked sea,
three feet from the high
wooden dock.
Drowning in turquoise,
     in black.

My daughter drowning also
    in my dream.
And I go down with her,
and with all the others,
    women of varnished faces.

Now my face sleeping
    the color of oyster shell
    underwater.
Her body curled around itself
    white,
      embryonic.
And there is light coming
    up around us from
    the sand ridges
of the ocean floor.
Underwater we are twins.
    No. She is my mother.
      No. I am my mother,
my womb water.

I am floating in birth,
    in the night side
like aster under
    its fleshy petals
like the orchid hot
    in a luxury of ice.
Slipping over the compass rim
    the drowning wind and moon
pass into the mouth of water.

In this blue room of the body
     I learn the edges,
         the shape,
the writing on the walls of dream.
And wake
     holding in my mouth darkness,
the essence of ambergris cast
        onto a shore.

RIDING TRAINS

My son sleeps   with his head   on my lap
This I can hold   a small station   by the cindered track
Our train racks on   through Pennsylvania   and the rank air
of New Jersey   I grow drowsy   lay my head back
into love   then the shadows   thousands crawling
from old boxcars   (gold fillings   lampshade skins)
and if you had   a child to hide   if his life   began to spill
down your breasts   could you hide him   inside a body
cut a place in   one just dead   (suffocation   malnutrition)
keep him breathing   keep him saved   as if love
meant anything   He holds my hand   awakened now
as we dive through   the Hudson Tube   under water
shadow light space   the womb pushed down   expelling us
until we slide   the other side   the hard light
coming down   between us.

BREAKING SILENCE

It has taken us forever
to get this far—
Mitchell, South Dakota,
the Corn Palace,
that parched Russian mosque
held together with corn cobs,
corn silk hair, corn honey,
the sexual tassels sweating
down on the sweaty tourists.

We are too tired to assault
any more of plains and sky,
any more of the anonymous farms,
the predictable signs—
tennis court,
swimming pool,
vacancy.
There is a vacancy inside our bodies.
It is July, 98 degrees,
and the heat rolls through us
like quicksilver.
We take what we can get.

But everything is broken,
or nearly broken—
door latches,
promises, a man's work,
and the tile in the bathroom
curls off like old skin.
We carry towels to the pool,
my daughter and I,
our pubic hair singing
inside our suits like corn silk,
yellow and red and gold.

And we ride the slippery aquamarine slide
with a curve halfway down
like a badman's heart
that shoots us off into a deepness
where we must know how to swim,
because in Sioux country
this is the Mariana Trench.
But we can swim and do,
dog-paddling, kicking,
getting our breath,
filling our lungs with corn dust.

Tomorrow we will go on,
through Mission, a rebel enclave,
past the white-crossed cemeteries
missionaries built,
past Russel Means going to jail
for inciting to freedom,
for teaching children how
not to sink,
their black hair flowing out
around them like cilia.

We will cross into Nebraska,
drive through Valentine
where the highway plunges down,
a bloodline into the Sand Hills,
where the telephone poles rock
like ghosts in the wind.
We will arrive finally at McCook
in time for the 90th birthday
of Winona Metheny, great-grandmother,

girl-child of homesteaders, and
survivor of silences
who has a story to tell
as long as the long wind rushing
across these plains.

WHAT'S LEFT OF THE PILGRIMS
AT PROVINCETOWN

There is a museum with a painting
of the right whale rising to the water's surface
after the kill.
Buoyed up in a great rush of air
he floats past death like the witches of Salem
who were tied with stones
and thrown into a pond.

There is a tableau,
Pilgrims coming ashore,
stealing basketed corn buried
near the beaches.
They carry muskets on their strict shoulders.
Behind them, the *Mayflower* settles
into the harbor, and the stranger,
Peregrine, is born.

And there is Commercial Street
now three hundred years later
where Provincetown lulls under its summer mask,
souvenirs and sex,
and all the suntanned bodies,
the seekers and the caught.

And there are the fishermen
docking in a harbor of sighs.
And the tuna, cod,
and the private shells of the soft boned sea
who do not believe in anything
that is not water.

VISITING THE MAYO CLINIC

Both clothes (the outer garment of the body) and illness (a kind of interior décor of the body) became tropes for new attitudes toward the self.
—Susan Sontag, *Illness as Metaphor*

Suffering laps the edges of this town
like a lake that has been diseased
for many years.
But nearly everyone is
impeccably dressed,
everyone neat, new-pressed,
showing no frailty in the elevators,
keeping whatever it is that crouches
inside the body locked up.

There are only a few
who break through their disguises.
A woman in the lobby,
her hands spread in front of her
like pink fish encased
in a clear plastic bag.
And a few old men,
nervous in their suits
beside their suntanned, healthy wives.

Still how gracefully we all fold ourselves
like water lilies
into the chairs placed for waiting.
How easily the petals of our breathing
rise and fall.

And now I want to sleep.
I want to close my eyes on it,
finger the antique bone that is in my jaw,
and dream only of the next appointment.

A LIGHT IN THE DOORWAY

Anything approaching us we try to understand, say,
Like a lamp being carried up a lane at midnight.
—Norman Dubie, *In the Dead of the Night*

It is late afternoon
just beginning to lose light.
This is the graveyard of the day
when you think you will not move again
either forward or backward.
And it is raining, slowly.
The reflections on the road
are like images on a seal's back
washing through a black wave.

Still my father-in-law drives,
nervously, carefully,
as he has all his life.
And he has little to say
as the car tires disappear into
these reflections
as into a drama,
then reappear on the other side
like an audience clapping.

Along the way a door is opened to a house
through which pale light comes
like that which comes from the underwings of moths.
A man has just entered the house,
has just come home from killing something.
He carries a black lunchbox
into which he has put the final tones
of the afternoon.

He loves his children who leap toward him
through this shaft of light.
He loves his wife standing with white dishes
like wafers of love in her hands.
His shoulders are damp with rain.
And with sea water.

In this ceremony he has left the door open
so that the other lives that pursue him
may come or go as they wish.

PILGRIMAGE

I. Toward Fremont

We pass over the Missouri from Council Bluffs
on a steel arch anchored to the flood plain.
And then we fold
into the quilted hills of eastern Nebraska,
into the texture and contour,
the wedding quilt of furrows
made by men who have married land.

U.S. 30 is a narrow ribbon
banding the Platte River.
We are going west into discovery,
into the soft muscle of a woman's womb.

II. McCook

This is the esplanade
to the Rockies.
In the illusion that is America
the 60's arrive here late.
Long-hairs at the swimming pool
peddle dope outside the chain link fence.
And a woman plays catch with her men,
her body trotting to the hard bed
of country-western music.

We stay with your grandmother five days.
She lives alone,
a widow in her widow's house.
Mementos of the trainman
crash around her basement
where we sleep fitfully
in the middle age of marriage.
But she appears, at 89, as calm and permanent
as the rain that comes nightly.

III. Leaving North Platte

After one week
Nebraska blows away in front of us.
Ground clouds puff north
to the Dakotas.
I welcome the highway,
and the rolled Sand Hills
forever changing themselves with wind.

You sit hunched over the map,
a man tracing the lost outlines
of buffalo herds
that once stretched north to south
like spiked thistle
rubbing against each other.

I know it is the energy of loss
that gets us from there to here.
Rotted farms with a legacy
of broken women grow down
beside fields of stiff grain.

Our children in the back
watch out the window
for a sign of grace.

PITT POETRY SERIES
Ed Ochester, General Editor

Milne Holton and Paul Vangelisti, eds., *The New Polish Poetry: A Bilingual Collection*

David Huddle, *Paper Boy*

Shirley Kaufman, *The Floor Keeps Turning*

Shirley Kaufman, *From One Life to Another*

Shirley Kaufman, *Gold Country*

Ted Kooser, *Sure Signs: New and Selected Poems*

Abba Kovner, *A Canopy in the Desert: Selected Poems*

Paul-Marie Lapointe, *The Terror of the Snows: Selected Poems*

Larry Levis, *Wrecking Crew*

Jim Lindsey, *In Lieu of Mecca*

Tom Lowenstein, tr., *Eskimo Poems from Canada and Greenland*

Archibald MacLeish, *The Great American Fourth of July Parade*

Peter Meinke, *The Night Train and The Golden Bird*

James Moore, *The New Body*

Carol Muske, *Camouflage*

Leonard Nathan, *Dear Blood*

Sharon Olds, *Satan Says*

Gregory Pape, *Border Crossings*

Thomas Rabbitt, *Exile*

Belle Randall, *101 Different Ways of Playing Solitaire and Other Poems*

Ed Roberson, *Etai-Eken*

Ed Roberson, *When Thy King Is A Boy*

Eugene Ruggles, *The Lifeguard in the Snow*

Dennis Scott, *Uncle Time*

Herbert Scott, *Groceries*

Richard Shelton, *The Bus to Veracruz*

Richard Shelton, *Of All the Dirty Words*

Richard Shelton, *The Tattooed Desert*

Richard Shelton, *You Can't Have Everything*

Gary Soto, *The Elements of San Joaquin*

Gary Soto, *The Tale of Sunlight*

David Steingass, *American Handbook*

David Steingass, *Body Compass*

Tomas Tranströmer, *Windows & Stones: Selected Poems*

Alberta T. Turner, *Learning to Count*

Alberta T. Turner, *Lid and Spoon*

Cary Waterman, *The Salamander Migration and Other Poems*

Marc Weber, *48 Small Poems*

Bruce Weigl, *A Romance*

David P. Young, *The Names of a Hare in English*

David P. Young, *Sweating Out the Winter*